Journey to Azelfafage

BY ANNE K. NAGEL

Nagela Press

Anchorage

Journey to Azelfafage

Library of Congress Control Number 2013903893
ISBN 978-0-9889676-0-1

Published in the United States by Nagela Press, P.O. Box 210036 Anchorage, Alaska, 99521-0036.

The publisher is not responsible for websites or website contents that are not owned by the publisher.

Cover art courtesy of NASA, ESA, and The Hubble Heritage Team (STScI/AURA).

This book is dedicated to Lovers and Poets everywhere.
Most especially to "B" and "J" – you know who you are.

TABLE OF CONTENTS

Introduction:

Azelfafage is a star in the middle of the Cygnus constellation. Cygnus means Swan. The myths of mortals being transformed into majestic swans are powerful literary symbols of the drab and mundane becoming something extraordinarily unique. *Journey to Azelfafage* alludes to the swan, and the changes in my life that inspired these poems. In them, words are transformed into something to make the mind pause, or make the spirit take flight.

Each poem is a step on my journey. They are presented chronologically with a short explanation of where I was and what I was facing at that point in my life. These verses gave me something positive to think about, and allowed my imagination to fly free when I felt hindered. If the ups and downs that inspired each of these creations can give just one person a different perspective or a push to keep going, then the apprehension of revealing a little bit of who I am in these pages is worth it.

I've been fond of the stars since I was young. The photographs of the galaxies have inspired me and lifted my spirit. Watching the successes and failures of space exploration gave me motivation and food for thought. I realized from an early age that I would never be an astronaut. I am 4'6" and hearing impaired, yet space exploration still excites me. I resist labels because they are hindering and misleading. A label makes it too easy to dismiss anything else the person could share. We all have the capacity for the transformation of the swan.

In my life, I have learned some important lessons: success and failure are significant, but the determination to try is more important. We can do something therapeutic for ourselves and others when we write down what we felt and how we overcame our obstacles. We can initiate healing when we write about the people, places, and things that inspire or challenge us.

I had to think long and hard before deciding to publish this. I hope that other people who are also facing challenges will know they aren't alone. We do matter, and we can succeed.

Anne K. Nagel

Anne K. Nagel

WHAT MIGHT HAVE BEEN

What might have been will never be,
it withers now, and dies.
Tomorrow's whispered mystery
fades in gloomy skies.
The sun that once kissed all I saw,
turns fickly away,
and summer, once so dewy fresh,
turns suddenly to gray.
The flowers, once so full in bloom
are drooping, growing old.
That which once was warm and free
turns hard and icy cold.
What might have been can never be,
It is withered now, and dying.
When I see it happening,
I cannot help my crying.

Anne K. Nagel

The Story Behind "WHAT MIGHT HAVE BEEN"

This poem was written in 1972. I had graduated high school that June. Around that time, my father got a job in Alaska. I wanted to stay in Washington State, where I had grown up, and go to college there. That didn't happen. Family pressure was put on me and I was forced to make the move with my parents and younger sister. I felt like I had been robbed of more than opportunities - I felt I'd lost my future and my hope.

Like the rest of his generation, my father was very traditional and orthodox. He felt that, as the head of the family, he could make these decisions with no discussion. What I wanted simply didn't factor into the matter.

At this time, I didn't title most of what I wrote. Before I became comfortable with my poetry, all I did was write down the year in which I wrote it. The title "What Might Have Been" came to me later, when I thought about the many things I could have done, or should have done. Suppose I had rebelled? What would my life have been like if I had stayed in Washington? If I had remained, where would my poetry be?

The fast approach of winter in Alaska was shocking. This only deepened my sense of loss. As I composed this piece, I kept being drawn to the imagery of things that have come to an end. I found myself thinking of a flower bud that was formed too late to bloom in the brief Alaskan summer. I struggled to make sure that each succeeding image would drive home the feeling of sadness at something cut short without mercy.

I still get sad when the summer's flowers die off. At the first frost, it's easy to anticipate the long winter that is just around the corner. Snow and ice in Anchorage will last from October through April. This poem shares a similar sense of melancholy with "Autumn," which I wrote before fully assimilating the reasons for my unhappiness.

AUTUMN

Sky of stormy hue
warms under sun's attentions;
Autumn touches Earth.

Gray geese start their flight
heeding nature's inner call;
Winter at its birth.

Trees now shed their leaves,
as golden tears of mourning
show the summer's worth.

Anne K. Nagel

The Story Behind "AUTUMN"

This poem was written in late 1972 about my difficult transition to Alaska.

Haiku appeals to me. I learned about it in high school and I liked the challenge of the structure, rhyme, and rhythm. Each of these three verses is in the Haiku style, though they may not adhere to the strict standards for that form. It was interesting to make all three parts work together to shape the larger work. I've never seen something like this in anything else I've read.

The poem originated on an overcast autumn day, when the sun's rays briefly turned the dull gray clouds a bright silver color. The ever-changing interplay of sun and shadow on the Chugach Mountains was a reminder that things change, whether we want them to or not.

I felt sad when watching the all-too-brief respite of summer fade into the crispness of fall, and then plunge into the harshness of winter. Writing this verse was, in some way, making peace with my forced relocation. It wasn't what I wanted, but it was something that I had to deal with.

STATE OF BEING

If you open your eyes,
you'll see me anywhere:
in the vagueness of a mountain
blending into a dark winter sky at dusk;
in the full moon, its brightness
demanding to be noticed;
in a piece of music
floating in your memory,
the words only faintly remembered;
in the solitary vigil of a star
poking through a sky
bedecked with clouds.
I am these things, and they are me.
And when I'm gone,
and you see these things,
you'll know I haven't really left
completely.

Anne K. Nagel

The story behind "STATE OF BEING"

This poem was written in 1972. I eventually gave it the title "State Of Being" because it reflects the calm and contemplative state of mind that I had at the time it was created. Some of my later work is harsher, as you will later see.

This was written during my first winter. I can remember how the snowy mountains looked as the sun was going down. Daylight in the depths of an Alaskan winter lasts only about five-and-a-half hours.

The sun's fading light colored the mountains with a light pink hue against a deepening blue sky. As the sun set, the snowy peaks were soon bathed in a deep purple color that quickly deepened to black. The moon and stars filled the dark sky, and at least they brought me some happiness.

By this time, I was a bit more centered. The situation at home was getting settled. I didn't like it, but I was learning to live with it. Anyone who has had to deal with a forceful parent can understand why it was taking so long to find my balance.

Some of the images, like the mountains I reflected on, will always be with me. Did I write this because I really was beginning to adapt to life in a strange place? It was more like I was trying to assimilate the place, making it a part of *me* rather than becoming a part of *it*. I didn't know it, but my transformation was beginning.

TODAY

The winds sigh,
their unwelcome touch freezes.
Some flakes fly
on frosty winter breezes.
The geese soar
in a sky of powder gray,
and here,
just content to watch them,
I stay.
I do not mind
the cold and the freezing,
for just to be living right now
is pleasing.
We wait for tomorrow
and forget yesterday.
But moments, like snowflakes,
so soon melt away.
Though I know that at sometime
all things pass away,
I am still joyful that
I've had this today.

Anne K. Nagel

The story behind "TODAY"

This was written in 1972. My younger sister asked me for something because she was supposed to write a poem for an English class, and she couldn't come up with anything.

I can't even recall why I agreed to her request. I may have been looking for something to do, to pass the time. College was too expensive because I was considered an out-of-state student. That was a label I couldn't fight. It would take living there a year before I could qualify for the cheaper resident tuition.

This was a portion of my life spent in limbo, just waiting. Anyone who has ever been through it can understand how boring and tedious this year was for me. That's why the title evokes positive thoughts of a good day. No past. No future. Like the poem, life at home was just "today" with the daily routine. There was not much to look forward to. One day was much like another, and time passed slowly.

Living conditions in Alaska turned out to be harder than anyone in my family thought they would be. The oil pipeline was just getting started, and everything was expensive. Our family had just one car, so my mom and I spent a lot of time at home.

Spending that time with my mom at that point in our lives made me sympathize with her many frustrations, which were similar to my own. It was this free time, and this necessity to do something, that gave me the motivation to look at my situation and examine my feelings.

SOARING FREE

I'm free at last, and my soul can run
among the countless ways
that for so long I've only dreamed of running,
but never dared.
Those who knew me
(or thought, at least, they did)
knew only bits and pieces.
Locked away, hidden from closest inspection,
was a person, half dream, yet reality, too.
But people's words of contempt
and rigid domineering attitudes
are hard shafts, and their blindness
aims these shafts indiscriminately
to pierce my dreams one by one,
leaving only half a person.
Nevertheless, my soul,
if only for a while in my innermost thoughts,
can soar further than the stars
and more freely than an eagle.

Anne K. Nagel

The Story behind "SOARING FREE"

This poem was written in 1973. The frustration of the previous year of inactivity shows in this piece. There are no pleasant-sounding rhymes, no soothing rhythms, and no constant length of verse. That creates the feeling of disharmony I was trying to evoke. The situation made me feel stifled, suppressed, and trapped. The disassociated feeling that was projected in this poem overshadowed everything else in my life.

At this time, I started college. What might have been a time of new beginning was curtailed as my father decided I had to take something inexpensive, something quick - only a two-year degree for me. Men of his generation didn't think most women needed college. He once told me that I would be taking a job away from a man by getting a college degree.

He also had the idea that the firstborn takes priority. I'm a middle sibling, and he didn't want me surpassing my oldest sister. Some people, in their compassion, hold us back because they don't want to see us get hurt. Others hold us back because they hate to see us get ahead.

My short stature and hearing problems probably factored into my father's decisions. On some level, he really did doubt that I could hold down a regular job, or drive, because of my disadvantages. Anyone who has to live with such things does become used to them after a while. It's your version of normal, so you just move on. I didn't let my shortcomings stop me from going back to college after I got a job, and could pay for it, to take other courses.

Being female and being a middle child were two labels I would spend a good portion of my young life fighting. My poetry helped give me an outlet. It got me in touch with these inner thoughts. I did exactly what my father demanded. Eventually, I got a degree in secretarial studies from Anchorage Community College. It was traditional enough to keep him satisfied, and just quick enough to get me out into a job and on my own!

CAUSTIC

All at once I see your face.
Your face is what I see,
and when I see that face of yours,
a feeling sweeps over me.
Yes, a violent and inner urge,
imbuing my whole being
with just one overwhelming thought:
to *not* see what I'm seeing!

Anne K. Nagel

The story behind "CAUSTIC"

This poem was written in 1973. It encapsulates what I felt as I started college. My parents had no money to give me a car, as they had done for my older sister. It was a method of putting a roadblock in my way.

Getting to the college campus was an adventure, because in those days the bus system wasn't very reliable. Many times I stood in the freezing cold, waiting for a bus that never came, or that whizzed by because the driver didn't see me. But I got there.

Then there was the nightmare of registering for classes. It can be quite disconcerting to be a short person in a big room with tall people who don't always see you. Add to this the fact that I had a hard time hearing over the noise of everybody else. I can understand why some people like me avoid these situations if they can.

I had to stand in one line to sign up for a necessary class, only to find out it was closed. Then I had to stand in another to try to get something else at a time that would let me get to the campus without too many bus trips per day. And so on, in line after line. That would give anyone an attitude! After that, it was necessary to stand in line to get a student ID, too. And when I got the ID picture, the person taking the picture said my smile didn't reach my eyes. I wonder why! But instead of being snippy, I wrote this poem. This allowed me to explore feelings that would have been impolite to express to the individuals who evoked them.

It has been said by many writers throughout history that poetry is a kind of therapy. This was very true for me, especially in 1973. New inventions were being developed. The space race was on, and new things were being done for the first time out in space. College was a new thing for me. Like the space program's small steps into outer space, it was a small step outside of my comfort zone.

STAR GAZING

I will lie among the clouds
and count eternity
with those fathomless
and eerie shrouds
that keep all sight from me.
And when, at last, the clouds are torn,
I'll see the stars arrayed
and see the universe reborn
as space and time are stayed.
Then I'll wander through the stars
and know infinity
among those vast, mysterious depths,
unveiled endlessly.
I'll hear each star's revolution
and touch each star I see,
for the universe and its domain
all belong to me.

Anne K. Nagel

The story behind "STAR GAZING"

This poem was written in late 1973. It is one of my favorites. From this point on, much of what I wrote would have a cosmic theme. I needed inspiration in my life, and looking at the stars has always felt transformative.

I chose this style because, with it, I could make this poem longer than the Haiku structure would allow. It has a more flowing form, which gave me greater freedom in the word choices.

During this period, I just couldn't seem to achieve the focus or discipline to write in Haiku. It was a frustration that would last for many years. At this point, I focused on school and homework. Just trying to find a quiet place to study was hard. This was yet another of my father's roadblocks.

A few years ago, I read John Gillespie Magee, Junior's, "High Flight." His poem takes you from the ground into the sky, as with a runway or launch pad. After reading it, I imagined my poem as almost an extension of his, taking the reader from the sky out to the stars. Quite a flight, indeed!

JUPITER

Jupiter shimmers majestically
in the dark midnight sky.
The other stars, like courtiers,
stand in attendance nearby.

VENUS

Venus, the bright one,
at dawning and dark.
Her shimmering aura is
her special mark.

The sultry opulence of Venus
is seen at dusk and dawn,
when all the attending stars
have long since faded and gone.

MARS

Mars is cold fire,
a red opal in space,
whose orbit will transpire
to swerve from retrograde
and then go fast and straight.

Anne K. Nagel

The story behind "JUPITER," "VENUS," "MARS"

These three poems were originally written in 1974 and redone in 2006.

This was another cosmically inspired project that called for a trio of linked verses. Each one is a separate poem in its own right, though not in the Haiku style.

I bought myself a little telescope somewhere around the time I originally wrote these poems. It was just a small instrument, but it allowed me to look at the moon and the brighter stars. I even gazed at a comet or two. That telescope got my mind off problems and gave me a way around family restrictions. It allowed me to explore.

As I compiled all the poems, I wasn't sure that I should include these three. In spite of my effort, I felt the originals were more like a child's sing-song verse, so I reworked them. I feel the later versions are better. Even if our first effort fails, we should still try again.

It's important to find ways to lessen our hurts and feed our passions. That goes a long way toward making us better human beings.

WHERE AM I?

If you go out some starry night
and stand when the moon is pale and fair,
look toward the star with the brightest light.
I'm in that direction, just over there.

You'll have to look deeply into the sky
just before Earth's new day is forming.
You'll see my star hanging very high,
until its light joins the sun's at morning.

Anne K. Nagel

The story behind "WHERE AM I?"

This poem was written in 1974. It continues the cosmic theme. I revised it in 2005 and tweaked it. After 31 years, my skill had improved, and I wanted to share this better version with you.

At this point in time, I didn't feel quite so lost anymore. School was more of a known quantity and life began to settle into a routine. I enjoyed learning new things and being challenged in my college courses. They fed my mind. The astounding pictures of Jupiter which the probes sent back from space fed my imagination.

There is more of an "expectant" feel about this poem that reflected the new stability in my life. I felt like something was about to happen; as if the "light bulb" was about to switch on, and maybe soon things would click into place for me.

College was nearing the end, and I was mentally preparing for the next challenge and change in my life.

SPECTER

At night there is a specter,
a form all dark and gray.
Disturbing, yet familiar,
a shadow's interplay.

I'm the shadow on the wall,
just a fading dream I see.
The remnant of a future
now just a memory.

Too much and too little,
and it's time to pay the fee.
The deceptions and depressions
have taken their part of me.

For sleeping dreams or waking
aren't much on which to go.
And dreams and schemes are nothing
that give one much to show.

While too much and too little
have taken their part of me,
the deceptions and depressions
are how I pay the fee.

Anne K. Nagel

The story behind "SPECTER"

This was written in 1975. It sums up the mixed feelings that surged through my head and heart at that time. That year I graduated with a degree in secretarial studies at Anchorage Community College.

"Clerical help" would be yet another label to resist. I was able to add anthropology and sociology as electives, and that made me want more. Later, I would go back and take a few other college classes at night.

The idea of "karma," or of things coming full circle, just resonated with me. The mystical quality of it suggests the potential of that mythical swan that has never ceased to inspire me.

This use of "past and future" or simultaneity shows up in later poems more prominently because it took many years for me to reconcile my past with my future endeavors.

As I wrote this verse, I felt stuck somewhere in between. In the future, I would accomplish many things. I would leave home and become a capable adult. I would even embark on a career spanning thirty-seven years and deal with more complex data than I would ever have imagined. But all that was a future waiting to be written. From this point forward, the darkness would never remain bottled up inside without release because I would have my poetry to express it.

ALONE

I'm never going to take some guy's fancy,
I always take second place.
If it's a choice between me and another,
I always lose the race.

I get tired of taking a chance,
hoping I'm the one who will win.
It always turns out the same
and I'm alone again.

I keep hoping that I'll make it and
I'll have somebody's love.
But it's a dream always before me,
out of reach somewhere above.

Out of reach, far from my grasp,
then I wake up in the morning;
my hope and strength
just cannot last.

Anne K. Nagel

The story behind "ALONE"

This was written in mid-1985. This ten-year poetic drought was partly due to having started work in 1975 and having devoted my attention and energy to the job. I had also succeeded in my goal to go back and take some college classes at night for a while. The math and computer courses allowed me to work with the programmers (though I never became one myself) and let me take on more responsibility than the "clerical" label would encompass.

Our lives are unique individual journeys. We may not always know where we're going, but we are on an odyssey of change, whether we realize it or not. I started work as a civil service employee ten years earlier. That success was tempered by the loss of my mother to a sudden heart attack.

This form of venting or decompression is the greatest therapy that poetry can offer to the person who writes it. Letting those things out was good for me. Getting out of my father's house was good for me, too. Like the swan, I was coming in to my own and going through a transformation. I took on a lot more responsibility and accountability at work, and with my dad. Surmounting these challenges changed the way I viewed the world.

My job gave me enough financial freedom to have a car and condominium. Friends and family were somewhat surprised at just how independent I became. I don't blame them for having their doubts.

Those of us who have made peace with our disabilities need to appreciate that the rest of the world doesn't have our insight. The people around us don't always understand just how much we want to lead our own lives. We need to kindly let them know when we have these things under control.

I found the right car for me so that my size wouldn't be a problem. I bought a place I could afford. I paid my bills and got my groceries. Hearing aids, chair adjustments, and a few other things here and there allowed me to be good at my job without being a bother. Work, night courses, and the occasional date kept me busy during this transformative phase of my life. All of that was part of the inspiration for this poem.

STAR COMPANION 1

I love the feel of Romance,
I love the thought of Love.
I like to think you're not a dream
my imagination has made up.

I need to believe you do exist,
and that you will be here,
at another day and time
and in some other year.

Because we have some things to learn
we must now be apart.
But there's a place made just for you
in the recesses of my heart.

Faintly, in the deepness of my soul,
a trace of you remains.
Ethereal as the starlight,
it is real just the same.

Perhaps we have been lovers
on some distant, future moon,
or maybe we have yet to meet
at some ancient Pharaoh's tomb.

Yet I feel our spirits moving,
like the stars in celestial flow,
in the timeless cosmic dance
through which our souls must go.

So I'll wait, dear Star Companion,
until the dance is through,
and all the past-and-future turnings
bring me back to you.

Anne K. Nagel

The story behind "STAR COMPANION 1"

This poem was written in 1989. I had more control of my destiny. My father was still a part of my life, in his own uncompromising way. At this time, he was beginning to slip away due to Parkinson's disease, which is a neural-degenerative disorder that affects the human brain.

This poem has a smooth flow and bright theme that was appropriate for my mood at that time. The cosmic elements are more pronounced because I wanted to emphasize the ethereal aspects in the poem.

I purposefully positioned the old and new, the past and future, together to give a "time-flow" feel to the poem. The idea of going backward or forward in time, and the concepts of past lives or reincarnation, fascinated me. I became aware of the works of Edgar Cayce at about this time. I wanted this piece to show the influence of those ideas. These concepts were explored further in "Star Companion 2" and "Star Companion 3."

These three poems and their transitions through time did make me think of my father and his declining mental faculties. There were days when he was "here," and other times when he was somewhere in the distant past.

I could've abandoned him. It would have been easy to just not answer the phone. Who would blame me, if they knew the truth? I wanted to be a better person than that, so I remained with him through to the end, which wouldn't come for another ten years. I'm glad I made that choice.

STAR COMPANION 2

In the domain of the Cosmic,
my life is just a sigh.
Like a candle in the celestial night,
soon it will flicker and die.

Now the light of my spirit burns low,
and the cosmic winds begin to blow.
Oh, Star Companion, will you meet me?
When?   And how will I know?

Could it be we've prearranged
some secret lover's code?

Oh!   Long-sought Companion!

I sometimes think of you
resting in some lovely place.
But why must you linger there?
How I long to see your face!

Must I wait another lifetime?
The cosmic winds blow cold
and I fear I'll leave this life
not having you to hold.

Anne K. Nagel

The story behind "STAR COMPANION 2"

This poem, written in 1990, is the companion piece to "Star Companion 1." It continues the past-and-future theme. I gravitated to this idea because it gave a dreamy, mystical, romantic feel to the poem. It was my way of setting my imagination free for a while.

I was deliberately seeking the dreamy, mystical, and romantic to offset the analytical requirements of work. My job was entering and doing quality control of very technical - and very dull - data. I found a certain amount of pleasure in making sure it was correct. Yet I couldn't escape the feeling that nothing but spreadsheets, and no dreams, were making me feel dead inside.

The abrupt break in the rhythm in the middle of the piece stops the flow, as though one were crying out to the "Star Companion," so to speak. Or, perhaps I should say, so to write. In this piece I am playing with the poetry even more, as you can see.

SONG OF THE KNIGHT

With a sword in my hand,
I seek to vanquish the foe.
But, truth to tell,
what do I know?

I think that I'm happy,
with visions of Right.
My heart set on battle
and becoming a knight.

I practice hard with the sword,
though the older knights jest.
Still, I practice on
to become the best.

I practiced the sword,
my arm grew strong.
No one said a word
as I followed along.

Out through the wasteland,
the desert grows hot.
If some of them grumble,
I vow I will not.

But the wasteland is no place
in armor to fight.
In the heat of the desert
Valor melts just like ice.

And now they have us,
comrades die one by one;
at the place of "The Horns"
there is no place to run.

Anne K. Nagel

So I pick up a weapon,
I slash and I slay.
I vow in my heart
I won't run away.

Though my body grows weary,
I continue to try.
I must keep on fighting.
To stop is to die!

To this very day
I'll never forget
the view from my visor,
the sand and grim sweat.

Even now I remember
the rough sandy rise,
the last sight I saw
with those dying eyes.

With a sword in my hand
I died there that day,
at the Horns of Hattin,
a lifetime away.

The story behind "SONG OF THE KNIGHT"

This was written in 1991. It continues the "past-future" theme that has become my favorite subject. The origin of this work is unusual, even for me. It symbolizes much of what I believe in. I'm proud of the pure artistic energy that inspired it.

At one point, I had a conversation with someone who was active in the Society for Creative Anachronism (SCA). He was describing a historic encounter between two armies that actually happened during the Crusades in the Middle East.

As we talked, I had a vision of that battle, and a rocky rise as seen through the restricting view of a helmet's visor, as though I were really there. The imagery was so potent and provocative that I was compelled to write it down.

Even though the poem depicts what would be a traumatic incident, there is no hatred in it. The strongest emotions it evokes would be the desire to overcome all odds at the beginning, and the determination to continue despite all odds toward the end. Any negative emotions, like fear or hate, have been discarded with death's transformation.

At the heart of this epic verse is the resolve that I learned from all the good and bad things I experienced in my life.

It is the most powerfully evocative piece I've written and my lengthiest work so far.

Anne K. Nagel

STAR BIRTH

The Galaxy sings to her children
as they are being born,
and she brushes them a kiss
as their nebular blankets are torn.

In the star clusters of Orion,
the stellar wind-songs are played,
and her children stand naked in space
all fresh, still in stardust arrayed.

I've been part of the stellar ballet
of Gravity, Neutron and Light
that press at me, pull me away,
and steer me through the night.

The Galaxy sings her song,
and she's singing it now to me.
My soul and spirit are caught up
in her celestial harmony.

The Galaxy mourns for her offspring
as they die in the celestial night.
But their last kiss to the heavens
continues the ballet of light.

Anne K. Nagel

The story behind "STAR BIRTH"

This poem was written in 1995. It was inspired by the images of the dust pillars in M16. That is certainly an awe-inspiring sight, and one that captured my imagination.

In this poem, the "children" are the new stars being born. The "nebular blankets" are the dust clouds that surround each newly forming star until the "T-Tauri" winds begin at the igniting of the star's internal nuclear forces and the surrounding dust is blown away.

From an astronomical point of view, when a star is born, the internal nuclear forces create heavier elements. When it dies, the star's explosion distributes these richer elements into the surrounding area of space. This causes "clumps" of matter to form, creating new stars from this richer material. Death becomes transformed into Light and Life.

THE SEQUENCE OF MY LIFE

The days of my youth, so free of care,
gave way to growth and strife.
Now, I am like a solitary river.
Like the river, I'm ever in transition.

I have achieved experience.
Like the river, I have borne a lot:
seasons of change,
the cold of people's indifference,
power,
drought.

And I still know the rebirth of resolve,
like the return of spring.
My power still flows.
Where am I going?

As time passes from the Spring of Youth
to the flowing, golden Autumn of my Wisdom,
I will know.

Anne K. Nagel

The story behind "THE SEQUENCE OF MY LIFE"

This was written in early 1995. It refers to my mother, who died in 1985. There is no soft rhyme or rhythm in this piece, yet it is less discordant than other pieces I've written. The river is me. It perseveres just like I do, even through a drought of creativity.

The images are intended to be hopeful and strong rather than melancholy. This verse brings to mind quiet endurance, which makes me think of the unobtrusive strength my mother had as she dealt with my father's many moods.

Release of grief is nothing to be ashamed of. It is a necessary thing. I reached a stage in my life's journey where this poem and its release were possible only because I kept going, even through the bad times.

The loss of a parent is hard for any of us. Everyone processes that emotional impact in different ways. I may never know just why it took me ten years to write this, but I can say that it was the right thing to do at that moment. I was old enough, wise enough, and ready to reveal my thoughts, which I could not have done earlier.

TIME AND THE FLAME

Time and the flame.
Both are only ephemeral.
The heavy hand of time is seen
as the brightest flame becomes
only wafting smoke;
a fragile memorial.
And today becomes
only a fleeting memory.

Anne K. Nagel

The story behind "TIME AND THE FLAME"

This moody piece was written in late 1995. I was continuing to experiment with using no rhythms or rhymes. This elegy is intended to explore the temporary nature of our existence.

I was still preoccupied with the transitory motif. My mother's death figured prominently in the last poem I wrote, and I was now confronted by my father's worsening Parkinson's disease.

That once very outspoken man was suffering from aphasia, meaning that he could no longer translate his thoughts into words that any of us could understand. As many times as I had clashed with him in the past, this turn of events was disturbing to me for several reasons. It was a form of being trapped. Poetry allowed me a form of outlet and communication that I needed and craved. To be unable to express any thoughts is a horror I'd rather not contemplate.

MOM

I had a dream about you last night.
From the horror of a gas truck
skidding sideways on a crowded road,
to a crowded eating place with tacky tables and chairs.

Someone took my hand and led me from the chaos.

Sitting facing away from me, on a couch
with Dad, you spoke to me of someplace pleasant,
with the wind's sound through the evergreens.

In your gentle voice you said it would be so nice -
and it was; to hear you, to see you again.

Anne K. Nagel

The story behind "MOM"

This jagged poem was written in late 1995. It was based on a disturbing dream about my mother. The trauma of her passing still affected me, even after ten years.

She didn't really die in a fiery explosion as the dream depicted, though her real-world death was terribly sudden. This was probably just another symptom of my delayed release of grief. It could also be indicative of a feeling of being out of control. With my mother dead, I was left alone to try to take care of my father, who was becoming increasingly debilitated from Parkinson's disease.

No two life journeys are the same. We must play the hand we are dealt, and the outcomes of our individual trials are never quite the same, though they can be eerily similar.

I knew when it was time to let go of the grief. I did it in a fashion that worked for me. A lesson to draw from this is to let the past be in the past. That insight helped me to dig deeper in to my concerns over brief existence.

ALIEN VISTA

There's a place along a silver shore,
against which calming azure wavelets pour.

The crystal forests, towering high,
spread their jeweled limbs against a copper-colored sky.

With the teasing of each Aeolian breeze,
comes a spectral chiming from the iridescent trees.

Where ethereal moons whose rings, like gems,
are set amidst the glittering stars like diadems.

The stately rings, in all their majesty,
rain a blessing of stardust upon my love and me.

A treasured place with treasured company;
my mate, his people, mine for all eternity!

Anne K. Nagel

The story behind "ALIEN VISTA"

This poem was written in 1997, and goes back to a more flowing, softer style. This poem has a lot of beautiful, happy imagery.

It is interesting to think about that year. In 1997, my father was moved in with my brother. This took a lot of pressure off me. The more fluid style may well have resulted from the release of stress his move provided.

With my dad settled in with my brother and his wife, I could turn my attention to the changes in my life. What was I going to do, now that I wasn't needed anymore?

Before this, I had precious little opportunity for outside activities or socializing. Now there was time, but what did I want to do, and with whom? I had to start getting my life back together, which I did.

STAR COMPANION 3

Star Companion;
I've searched the sky,
I've searched the faces.
I've looked in many eyes
and I've reached for many hearts,
looking for traces.
Traces of ... what?
A glimmer of love - just an idea.
A hint of hope;
a trace of you.
Why aren't you here?
I cannot find you.
Another cold day,
another cold year.
I cannot find you,
you are not here.

Anne K. Nagel

The story behind "STAR COMPANION 3"

This poem was written in 1998, and is the final portion of the "Star Companion" trilogy. It has little rhyme softening the lines. In it, there is a sense of waiting and wondering. There is no "happily ever after" just around the corner. In life, as in the poem, there were more questions than answers.

After my father's death, I was left to wonder about his final thoughts. Did he know he was dying? Did he have any regrets? Was there anything he wanted to say to me or anyone else before the end?

It may have been wrong to expect any regrets or justifications from him, even at that late date. My curiosity remains unsatisfied; however, my younger sister did say that toward the end, he called her by my name. Was he thinking of me?

In my own way, I was using poetry to let go of the past so I could embrace a better future. My poetry, combined with all the other educational and creative outlets I could now explore, played a small part in my transformation from grief-burdened offspring to confident daughter.

NOT A GEEK

The ethernet cable he wields with practiced ease;
a cyber-whip in his hands.

Gigabytes and power surround him
like a leather coat.

They bend to his will:
he's a techno-stud.

Anne K. Nagel

The story behind "NOT A GEEK"

This poem was written in 2001. It was inspired by a friend who is very much into technology. It has no rhyme or rhythm, but it is upbeat. Technological concepts are combined to form the images. The man and the computer come together and become one.

I like this poem because it shows that someone who is very technologically adept can be other things besides a geek: one can also be mysterious, even sexy. As I pointed out in the introduction, superficial labeling limits our perception of the person being categorized in such a limited way.

Computers were slow and clunky when I started working for a living. I learned to use them as part of my job. They were faster and cheaper by the time I wrote this piece.

I was reluctant to get a computer at first, and my friends didn't think I was actually going to do it. They even followed me around the store to see if I would! But once I made up my mind, I did it.

I was quite happy to buy a desktop PC for my own personal use when the prices came down to a reasonable level. It was yet another transformative event for me, although I could never be called very technologically adept!

NOT-QUITE-SPRING

Once-barren branches
show the season's first bounty:
a pussy willow pelt.

Winter's ornaments
become singing rivulets,
as icicles melt.

The hush of winter
is banished by the breezes.
Spring's first touch is felt.

Anne K. Nagel

The story behind "NOT-QUITE-SPRING"

This was written in 2001, before I moved from my apartment.

In this piece, as in "Autumn," I used the style of the three Haiku to build a larger poem and convey layers of images. I particularly like the happy descriptions. It is as though one is a hunter, searching for hidden traces of spring. The ornaments in the verse are the icicles that freely form as the late winter snow thaws.

The rhyme marks my return to the use of Haiku. It is quite a change from some of the more introspective pieces that I'd been writing. The release of pressure in my private life resulted in a happier, softer choice of words.

At that point, my life was changing. I had moved into an apartment a couple years earlier. Soon, I would start looking for a different place. I didn't know it, but the old pressures would slowly be replaced by other pressures in my life.

There would be more transformations. I was no longer the same, so work no longer fit like it used to. The old ways just didn't seem to apply any more. I was toying with the idea of writing more than just poetry.

In this poem, the "hunter" is searching for more than just signs of spring. I am the hunter, and I'm searching for a sign of what should come next.

EARLY SPRING

Fragile buds of spring
tenderly sprout on a branch
caressed by a breeze.

New life emerges,
reviving the blank landscape.
Winter slowly leaves.

Warmth returns, and light,
filtered softly through petals
on the ancient trees.

Anne K. Nagel

The story behind "EARLY SPRING"

This poem, written in 2005, shows an increasing happiness that comes with growing warmth and light.

The triple Haiku shows not only the awakening of the landscape, but also the awakening of my senses as spring finally arrives. It is filled with pleasing images of soft colors and lights and scents. My delight at these sensory pleasures is evident.

Many things were changing in my life. I bought my home in 2002, and was kept busy with it and work through the winter of 2004. I was motivated to write this while looking out through my living room window at the burst of colors peeking through the melting snow.

I looked back over my older poems and tried to recapture my interest in cosmic themes. That spark just wouldn't reignite, which worried me until I realized that my life's journey was requiring me - forcing me - to focus on other things.

That moment of insight marks a turning point in my life. All of my poetry from that day forward would be a mixed bag. Those verses and rhymes would be different because *I* was different. Like a mythical being on its way to being that swan I so admire, I was now ready for another transformation.

THE CREATION OF POETRY

As winter gives way to spring,
I am reminded of why I write.

Late winter's snow, so soon melted,
gives way to rivulets,
as a single word leads to more.

With pen to paper, in the early spring light,
I watch the ice give way,
like the previous
blockages in my mind.

The restrictions of winter
transform into the new
possibilities of spring-fed life.

The new grass, the new buds,
the new life, symbolize new
possibilities and spark new creativity.

This demands that I write.

Anne K. Nagel

The story behind "THE CREATION OF POETRY"

This was written in 2005. It depicts the restrictions I feel in winter, and how those restrictions seem to lift when spring comes. With spring's return, I feel an increase in creativity and peace.

The stanzas are not as abrupt as in some pieces. Despite the lack of rhyme, it is softer and more flowing than some of my darker pieces. This poem doesn't have the artistic and fanciful word-pictures of earlier poems. It is more grounded in reality - another transformation.

This was my way of using natural themes to evoke positive thoughts. A friend and fan suggested I gather these poems together. About this time, I started to take the idea of developing this book seriously.

It was just an idea at that point, nothing more. Leafing back through the pages in my notebook made me think that perhaps there was real value in what I'd written. It really did *demand that I write*.

I kept the idea in the back of my mind, never quite certain that I would actually do this. Who'd want to read it? What would I say? How do I make it say more than just poetry? The answers wouldn't come to me for another seven years.

CHAINED TO A DESK

Unshed tears and unrealized dreams.
My soul is bleeding,
bleeding for the unwritten verse.

Unsighed yearnings and unreached hopes.
My soul is chained,
chained by the need for poetry.

Boredom and unrelieved sameness,
my soul in search of a reason,
tortured for inspiration,
bereft of satisfaction.

Anne K. Nagel

The story behind "CHAINED TO A DESK"

This was written in the early summer of 2005. By that time, work was tedious and repetitive, with no outlet for creativity or initiative.

I had put a number of years' worth of work into collecting a lot of data and creating some spreadsheets. Then management deleted the files because they didn't understand the usefulness of the information.

The only relief was putting that pain into poetry. The repeating words mimic the repetitiveness of inputting the data, and the repetitiveness of trying to explain the importance of the information. That is why I didn't use the Haiku style.

I tried not to rock the boat at work. Doing so shows bad manners. I didn't want anyone to think that I was trying to take advantage of my disadvantages, which is easy to do in today's politically correct world.

As I wrote this poem, I understood that it was time to find ways to harness my anger and frustration. That meant figuring out what bothered me. Fix it or vent it, and get the anger out of my system.

That may sound good, but it wasn't easy. Women are not encouraged to be so forthcoming in the workplace when they have grievances. Mine were what you'd expect: unthinking coworkers and clueless management. It was hard to admit that "they" had gotten to me.

This truth needs to be shared so that other people like me can see for themselves that they are not alone, and their situation isn't strange or unusual. These are hardships that all of us encounter at some point in our careers.

Face it. Life isn't fair. But, like the swan, I did overcome. I did persevere. The poems in these pages don't tell you the whole story, but they say just enough to let others like me know *we* can get through circumstances like this, if *we* try.

WINTER

Somber thoughts descend
along with the setting sun,
yearning for the light.

A gash of brightness,
the horizon is swallowed
by encroaching night.

Darkening twilight.
A confined, unhappy mood,
too stifling to write.

Anne K. Nagel

The story behind "WINTER"

This was written in 2005. It is a companion piece to the other triple Haiku verses relating to the seasons.

This poem reflects the restrictive, almost claustrophobic, feeling I get as the winter sun sets. The thin line of light at the horizon swiftly dwindles, as though the darkness is closing in, and the long winter night descends.

Obviously, Anchorage's dark winter is not my favorite season. The winter twilight at the ending of the day is symbolic of the death of creativity and happiness, as the cold forces me to spend more time indoors.

It's not easy to live in Alaska. You've got to give yourself extra time when you go anywhere in the depths of winter. There's all the time you need to bundle up in heavy winter clothing, and to clean off the car before you can shovel the driveway. Then, you've got to drive slowly on the ice to reach your destination in one piece. Whether it was to the office, or back home, the destination was always to the same four walls. Overcoming harsh climates can be thought of as another test, or transformation.

If the other Haiku needed the nuances of the western flute, I feel that this one would require the austere tones of the traditional Japanese Shakuhachi to match the harsh Alaskan winter.

BOREDOM REIGNS SUPREME

Once I handled more.
Once my heart and soul were there.
Boredom's killing me.

My knowledge once reigned.
But now my hands are shackled
and I am useless.

Now I'm forgotten
and they ignore my warnings.
They deserve what comes.

Anne K. Nagel

The story behind "BOREDOM REIGNS SUPREME"

This poem was written in 2005. Like "Chained to a Desk," it shows my growing frustration with work. Data input may give one a paycheck, but it doesn't feed the soul.

During this timeframe, we were going through an increasing number of "reorganizations" at work and it no longer felt rewarding. It was another transformation. I surprised myself by turning to poetry so easily for the creative stimulation that I craved.

This presentation is arranged as three Haiku. As a trio, they encapsulate everything that made me unhappy. It was a little ironic to me at the time that some of the new technology that I liked so much was making me obsolete. No matter how hard I tried, there was just no keeping up with it.

Changing focus at work, changing priorities, changing philosophies, and changing technology can cause us to feel lost, without purpose or direction. The temptation is there to wallow in self-pity.

I didn't want to give in to that torment. It took hours of effort to think past all the things that were bothering me, to focus on the right frame of mind so that I could *let this out*.

I'd been writing short stories in my spare time, but the emotions I wanted to put on paper always seemed to come easier with poetry. Achieving the mental discipline to go beyond frustration so that I could paint this word-picture gave me something new to work with that I didn't fully appreciate at the time. It gave me satisfaction and purpose.

SUMMER

Such tranquility
to be outside in the shade
where cool shadows play.

The breezes carry
scents of flowers and mown grass
as clouds drift away.

While shadows lengthen,
the sprinkler's pace provides a
hushed end to the day.

-

Anne K. Nagel

The story behind "SUMMER"

This was done in 2005. It is the final companion piece to the other Haiku poems relating to the seasons.

It has a softer, more flowing style which corresponds to the easier, more relaxed feel of the season. Scenes of nature and bounty contrast with the harsh, barren images of "Winter." The inspiration for it came after turning on the sprinkler to water the lawn. I like to relate these verses to the soft, earthy tones of the oboe.

The satisfaction of writing the poetry began to contrast with the desolation I felt at work, where time passed slowly and I felt numb. I thought about everything I'd done to get this far in my life, and realized that I needed to re-think my future *again*. I felt lost. There didn't seem to be a pattern I could follow. *How did that swan survive the journey?*

That's when I knew it was time to begin planning for retirement. The goal would give me something to strive for. That's really what I wanted, something new to *achieve*.

ON A FALL DAY

Watching quietly,
falling leaves cannot be heard.
The world has no sound.

Anne K. Nagel

The story behind "ON A FALL DAY"

This was written in 2005, toward the end of a three-week-long illness. The original inspiration was about the ringing in my ears and the pressure in my head. I experience increased difficulty hearing when I get sick. I took a few of the images and put them into a single Haiku, making it more about silence than specifically about being sick.

The imagery of swirling leaves, watched from indoors, creates a feeling of separation from the activity. That separation is often experienced with deafness. This same separation was also deliberately used at work by not wearing my hearing aids. Using that separation kept me from being a part of unpleasant office drama.

The picture of the swirling leaves reminded me of the people at work, scurrying to look busy so they might get to keep their jobs. With my detachment, I let the chaos swirl around me like the leaves in the poem, and didn't get caught up in it.

ON A WINTRY DAY

The sun tries to conquer
the gray clouds,
but is vanquished, instead.

The wind carries the news
of winter's victory - snow.

Anne K. Nagel

The story behind "ON A WINTRY DAY"

This poem, written in 2006, portrays the late winter feel: the dreary gray sky hides the sun, and snow continues through March and April. I particularly like the word-picture of the last two lines, as the wet snow is wind-driven and stings my chilled skin.

By this time in the season, I am tired of snow. The constant battle to keep the car and parking pad cleared off is frustrating, and when the snow continues to fall, it's like Mother Nature is mocking me!

However, I got a shovel that fits me, and I used the shoveling as an opportunity for exercise and stress relief. I also used it as a mental workout. I employed the determination and perseverance that I had learned through all the years I've spent living and working in Alaska. I didn't stop till the entire parking pad and deck were done.

In the end, with sore muscles and a snow-free driveway, I could go to work with a clear conscience that I had worked out my aggressions on the snow, and not on anyone else!

MOOSE IN THE CITY

One day during my commute
I happened to see a city moose.
It was jogging along with my rush-hour group
like a businessman in a drab brown suit.
But the busy moose wasn't looking
to wrest financial gain,
just whatever piece of bark
his teeth could claim.
Instead of wanting to rise
on the corporate ladder,
he was just looking
to survive the winter.
How often are we like
this single-minded jogger,
and through life are we, too,
just a slogger?

Anne K. Nagel

The story behind "MOOSE IN THE CITY"

This poem was written in the spring of 2006. It may seem fanciful, but I actually did see a moose cantering along the side of the busy road during evening rush hour. The jogging moose was able to keep up with the slowed-down traffic for a short period until we left it behind.

The image of that animal, so intent on survival, stayed in my head. It seemed to symbolize so many of the things that were on my mind at that time. I felt caught up in the professional rat race like so many people do at a certain point in their lives.

It was at about this time when I received yet another label at work: management decided a number of us were surplus employees. I'd begun to figure I should start planning for retirement. Like so many career civil service employees, I soon discovered the actual *doing* of the thing is harder and takes longer than we think.

There was a lot to learn before I could start filing the retirement paperwork. I started slowly. I knew I would need the tenacity and fortitude that I had learned from many winters up here.

Retirement was still seven years away, so I had to find something that would ease my mind. Once again, poetry came to my rescue. There is no harm in having a little fun with the things that bother you, especially when that humor can be so therapeutic.

This poem may be trite, but the serious question at the end was one I kept thinking about. What was in my future? Was I heading toward a goal, or just biding time? Future goals, and staying above the despair and fear of reorganization, gave me a new direction.

FACING THE TRIALS

The dark clouds of my emotions
gathered in my mind;
then tears, like rain, flowed free,
when life sometimes seemed unkind.

Why the trials must be endured
can be confusing.

But in the present is my hope;
what happens now
is of my own choosing.

Anne K. Nagel

The story behind "FACING THE TRIALS"

This poem was written in the late summer of 2006, when a friend was experiencing an illness. I wrote it to give her some moral support and lift her spirits as she went through her trials. It is meant to convey strength and resolve, and we all have times when we could use some of that.

These verses represent many of the lessons I've learned since leaving home. The entire poem denotes the overcoming of adversity. Then, as now, I realize that what comes next depends largely on me and my choices.

People with disabilities are often told what they can't do, or why they shouldn't do something. We are so often urged to limit ourselves to more easily attainable goals. I could have taken that advice. If I had accepted the labels and settled for what was easy, I'd be a different person today.

This was the last verse I wrote before following through on my promise to retire, which I did at the end of 2012. This poem was created to inspire somebody else. In the end, it helped me, too. It symbolizes my resolve to overcome the challenges life can present, and epitomizes a lot of what I believe in.

The decision to publish this book took many years of thought. I started work on the first draft shortly before retirement. The final result is what you are now reading. It doesn't tell my entire life story, but it does preserve my most prized possession, which is the poetry in this collection.

Afterword:

In the story of Cygnus, Phaeton was struck by Zeus's thunderbolt and hurled in pieces into the river Eridanus. Later, the gods immortalized Phaeton by placing his shattered remains in the sky to form the constellation of the Swan.

From this legend we may take the lesson that we will experience life's highs and lows. We are to pick up the pieces and carry on, and in so doing we transform ourselves into something better.

Like the time-flow poems, our journey is now complete and we are brought back to where we started, though never quite the same. When my journey began, I was young, unsure, and untried. Now, I'm beginning a new journey in this second half of my life. I like to think that I am approaching wisdom and experience. Like the swan, I hope to be transformed into something beautiful!

I hope these words have given you wings to fly, and strength to continue your own journey, wherever it leads you.

Anne K. Nagel

About the Author:

Anne K. Nagel is retired and has lived in Anchorage, Alaska, since 1972. Poetry gives her the creative outlet and means of self-expression that work couldn't supply. Space, technology, and Nature are among her favorite themes.

www.ingramcontent.com/pod-product-compliance
Lightning Source LLC
Chambersburg PA
CBHW060658030426
42337CB00017B/2685